COOL CAREERS WITH

CAREERS FOR PEOPLE WHO LOVE TRAVELING

Morgan Williams

ROSEN
PUBLISHING

NEW YORK

Published in 2021 by The Rosen Publishing Group, Inc.
29 East 21st Street, New York, NY 10010

First Edition

Library of Congress Cataloging-in-Publication Data

Names: Williams, Morgan.
Title: Careers for people who love traveling / Morgan Williams.
Description: New York : Rosen Publishing, 2021. | Series: Cool careers without college | Includes bibliographical references and index.
Identifiers: ISBN 9781499468854 (pbk.) | ISBN 9781499468861 (library bound)
Subjects: LCSH: Tourism--Vocational guidance--Juvenile literature.
Classification: LCC G155.5 W551 2021 | DDC 910.23--dc23

Some of the images in this book illustrate individuals who are models. The depictions do not imply actual situations or events.

Manufactured in the United States of America

Find us on

Portions of this work were originally authored by Simone Payment and published as *Cool Careers Without College for People Who Love to Travel.* All new material in this edition authored by Siyavush Saidian.

CONTENTS

Introduction 4

CHAPTER 1
Heart-Pounding Travel 5

CHAPTER 2
Getting into the Air 12

CHAPTER 3
An Umpire's Life. 19

CHAPTER 4
Smooth Sailing 26

CHAPTER 5
Dedicated Deckhands 32

CHAPTER 6
Airborne Assistance. 39

CHAPTER 7
In It for the Long Haul. 46

CHAPTER 8
Showing Off. 52

CHAPTER 9
Camera Reporting 59

CHAPTER 10
Taking Measures. 65

CHAPTER 11
Performing on the Seas 71

CHAPTER 12
Group Traveling 77

CHAPTER 13
Working the Rails. 83

CHAPTER 14
Helping Others Get There. . . 89

Glossary. 94
For More Information 96
For Further Reading. 99
Index 100
About the Author 104

only do the planning take part in a few trips so they can learn about the places their customers will be visiting and the activities in which they will be participating.

It may seem like this job is fun and games, but adventure travel specialists face both physical and mental challenges. They need to have a lot of energy to be able to work hard all day long. They also need to be quick thinkers. People in this position need to be able to solve many types of problems—fast. They have to stay calm when dealing with emergencies. They need to assess situations to make sure conditions are safe for everyone in the group.

One of the most important parts of the job is working with people. Adventure travel specialists are with their group all day long for several days. Trips can sometimes even last for weeks or months. They need to be comfortable in front of a group. On the trip, you'll need to act as both a coach and a cheerleader, helping

Some people consider harsh environments and difficult obstacles things to be avoided. If you want to be an adventure travel specialist, you'll need to be very comfortable in these kinds of situations.

people to face difficult challenges. Adventure travel specialists also need to be good at working on a team. These teamwork talents will need to be communicated to the people on the trip so everyone can work together to have a great time.

EXCITEMENT ABOUNDS

There are a wide variety of adventure trips that need guides. Here is a small sample of the kinds of trips you could lead:

- **Land:** Backpacking, caving, dogsledding, llama trekking, mountain biking, snowshoeing, wildlife viewing
- **Water:** Fishing, kayaking, scuba diving, snorkeling, surfing, tubing, white-water rafting
- **Air:** Bungee jumping, hang gliding, hot air ballooning, parasailing, skydiving

There are no limits on adventure travel opportunities. If you choose this career, you could find yourself soaring through the air all over the world.

Adventure travel specialists do more than just lead people on great adventures. They also teach their clients something along the way. An ocean kayak guide might teach kayaking skills while they point out how to identify sea life along the way.

Adventure travel is sometimes called ecotourism. One of the goals of some adventure travel trips is to teach people to appreciate our environment and the plants and animals that live in it. This is especially true for people traveling to exotic locations worldwide. It's very important that travel specialists and their groups respect the natural world that's hosting them.

WHAT YOU NEED

Official training isn't always needed to become an adventure guide. The best way to prepare for a career in this field is to gain experience in the type of adventure you'd like to lead. If you'd like to become a white-water rafting guide, go on a rafting trip as a participant and watch what the guide does carefully. Another option could be to get a summer job working as an assistant to an experienced guide.

If you want to get more than just hands-on experience, wilderness or outdoor organizations often offer classes for aspiring adventurers. There are many groups that offer weeklong or monthlong classes during the summer. Some schools can even train you to become a guide.

As you gain experience, you should also work on the other skills you'll need as a guide: people skills and organizational skills. You may want to consider public speaking classes so you're comfortable in front of groups. Join a scouting organization or another group that will help you to build teamwork and outdoor skills. Take first-aid classes so that you'll be prepared for emergencies that can come up, and work on your outdoor cooking skills—most guides have to cook one or more meals a day, especially if you're taking clients somewhere remote. There's no definitive list of skills an adventure travel guide should have, so your best bet is to get as much experience and training as possible. That way, you'll be ready to tackle any challenges that crop up in the field.

WHAT TO EXPECT

There's a lot of variation in how much an adventure travel specialist can earn. People who work part-time or seasonally will make less, and work will only come around every so often. However, if you can land a full-time position, your ability to make good, consistent money will greatly increase. These positions can be hard to find, as much adventure travel happens during specific months of the year, and they offer their own set of challenges. Full-time adventure travel specialists can get burned out by having to take on too many trips too often.

Regardless of whether you find part-time or full-time employment in this field, you can expect to occasionally receive tips from your satisfied customers.

As people become more interested in both physical fitness and the environment, they'll be looking for activities that combine these interests. Adventure travel is just one area that's likely to expand. Though this industry can be highly competitive—especially when it comes to full-time employment—if you gather experience and sharpen your skills, you'll make yourself a great candidate for any jobs that come up.

CHAPTER 2

GETTING INTO THE AIR

Planes and jets of all shapes and sizes have fascinated people since their invention. Today, the military employs people to help launch and safely land fighter and surveillance planes. Stationed on aircraft carriers that travel around the globe, aircraft launch and recovery specialists have the exciting job of getting planes safely into the air and safely back down again.

WHAT YOU'LL DO

An aircraft launch and recovery specialist is in charge of making sure that all kinds of aircraft are able to both take off and land smoothly and safely. Working for the U.S. Navy, Coast Guard, or Marine Corps, aircraft launch and recovery specialists are stationed on aircraft carriers all around the world. They operate the catapults that launch these high-tech jets into the air at more than 150 miles (241 km) per hour. They direct the planes on the flight deck using hand

MILITARY TRAVELING

If you're interested in the military, but you don't think becoming an aircraft launch and recovery specialist is right for you, there are a lot of other options. Many of them even allow you to travel the world. Here are some other jobs you might like and their main duties:

- **Air crew members**: Operate equipment onboard aircraft.
- **Cargo specialists**: Deliver military supplies, weapons, equipment, and mail all over the world.
- **Flight engineers**: Monitor aircraft before, during, and after flights.
- **Seamen**: Operate and maintain military ships and submarines.
- **Vehicle drivers**: Transport troops, supplies, and fuel.

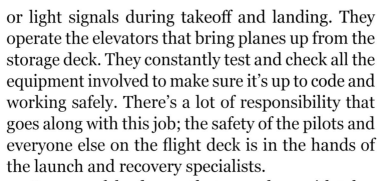

or light signals during takeoff and landing. They operate the elevators that bring planes up from the storage deck. They constantly test and check all the equipment involved to make sure it's up to code and working safely. There's a lot of responsibility that goes along with this job; the safety of the pilots and everyone else on the flight deck is in the hands of the launch and recovery specialists.

Because of the danger that goes along with takeoffs and landings, there are strict rules on the flight deck. Everyone must memorize a set of hand signals

so that they can communicate over the roar of the jet engines. Each crewmember has a specific job to do.

For a launch, one crewmember hooks the front wheel of the jet to the catapult. An engineer gives the plane a final check and then gives the pilot the signal to power up the engine. The launch officer gives a signal to the catapult offi- cer. They push a button and the 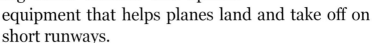 jet goes speeding into the air. Of course, before any of this takes place, everyone must be clear of the jet and the jet's exhaust.

Though many aircraft launch and recovery specialists work on military aircraft carriers, some work at landing sites near combat zones. If you're working on land, you could find yourself install- ing crash barriers and special equipment that helps planes land and take off on short runways.

WHAT YOU NEED

As long as you're qualified, a career in the military is one of the best opportunities around. Military positions can vary wildly, but they'll all train you to

Aircraft launch and recovery specialists have a tough job, but they keep at it because they experience satisfaction each time they help guide a plane during takeoff.

acquire a useful set of skills. You don't have to have any previous experience to join, and many positions don't require a college education. With nothing but a high school diploma, you can advance within the military, or you can get a job in the civilian workforce after you've finished active duty.

Before you get on the runway, you'll have to go through a lot of training and education. You'll also have to take an aptitude test to make sure this is the right job for you within the military.

To get started in the military, you need a high school education and you must be 17 years of age or older. You also must be a U.S. citizen or a lawful permanent resident. Before you join, try talking to a recruiter. Check local social media sites and official information to find a recruiter near you. This trained specialist will discuss your options with you. They'll also talk to you about

taking the Armed Services Vocational Aptitude Battery (ASVAB). This test evaluates your strengths and then gives you a list of career paths in which you might do well.

If you decide that walking a military path is right for you, the first thing you'll encounter is basic training. This difficult process gets you ready for service over the course of several months. An aircraft launch and recovery specialist will receive further weeks of education after basic training. During this time, you'll learn about how planes take off and land and how to operate the specialized landing and take-off gear found on an aircraft carrier.

After being trained, you'll begin your work as an apprentice, moving around all the stations on an aircraft carrier. You'll also learn how to repair and maintain equipment. If you're successful in your career, you could move up to crew supervisor or flight deck supervisor.

If you'd like to get a head start on the path toward becoming an aircraft launch and recovery specialist, taking classes in shop mechanics in high school may help you. You can also try talking to recruiters or other people in the military about what the job is like. They can tell you more about what to expect.

WHAT TO EXPECT

There are nearly 1.5 million members of the U.S. military. Of these, more than 10,000 are aircraft launch and recovery specialists. Needless to say, career paths in the Army, Navy, Air Force, and Marines aren't difficult to find. As long as you have the skills needed to supervise aircraft—and you're willing to work hard every day—you'll be able to find yourself working on an aircraft carrier that sails all over the world.

Though military life isn't for everyone, a career in the armed forces offers great benefits. As a government employee, you'll be given a predetermined salary that increases regularly. You'll also receive bonuses if you advance in rank, but military compensation doesn't stop at your paycheck. Military personnel also have access to full health benefits, paid leave, and your food and housing are paid for. Even without a college degree, if you want to become an aircraft launch and recovery specialist, you can find great compensation in this military career.

CHAPTER 3

AN UMPIRE'S LIFE

If you've ever watched a baseball game—at any level—you know that the umpire has an important job on the field. Like any on-field official, baseball umpires shoulder a lot of responsibilities, and they have to be ready to make quick, accurate judgments about rules and results. Of course, they must do all this while standing in front of hundreds, thousands, or even tens of thousands of fans. Whether an umpire's decision is met with loud boos or roaring applause, they have to know that the call they made on the field was the right one.

WHAT YOU'LL DO

An umpire's main duty is to make sure that players follow the rules of the game. Umpires also keep official records and take care of any arguments that come up during the game.

One of an umpire's most important skills is being able to concentrate. Baseball may seem slow on TV,

In addition to a thorough knowledge of baseball's rules and procedures, an umpire must have sharp eyes and strong concentration. The game's officials are responsible for making sure everything runs smoothly, safely, and fairly.

but there's no time to let your mind wander when you're on the diamond. Action happens fast, and even blinking at the wrong time could mean you miss something.

An umpire also needs to remain calm and professional at all times. Coaches, players, and fans are all passionate about the game, which can make calling a runner out an intimidating prospect. However, a good umpire knows that getting the call right is more important than listening to the crowd cheer.

During the baseball season, umpires will travel a great deal. Professional umpires in the major and minor leagues typically have their travel expenses and meals paid for. Most umpires stick within the United States, but some leagues do travel for international exhibition games, and if you're lucky, you may get to officiate them.

Umpires have to deal with many of the same things that players do. Games are often scheduled on weekends and evenings—sometimes even on holidays. Most games are held outside, regardless of whether it's very hot, very cold, or a bit rainy. Umpires are on their feet for the whole game, which commonly lasts around three hours. There's a lot of physical stress that goes into officiating, but—like players—umpires will have the winter months off after the end of baseball season.

WHAT YOU NEED

Most umpires get their start by working games at middle schools, high schools, or local recreation centers. People of all age levels, all across the United States, play baseball, and every game needs a fair and professional umpire.

To get started at this level, talk to local officials and contact associations such as the National Association of Sports Officials. As you start working amateur games like these, you'll not only improve your officiating skills, you'll also get the chance to see whether this career is right for you. Once you've gained some good experience—and you want to take the next step—you can try to move up to working college games.

As soon as you think you're ready to become a professional umpire, you'll need to get official training. There are two schools for aspiring pros: the Harry Wendelstedt Umpire School and the Minor League Baseball Umpire Training Academy. These training programs offer courses to talented

Because umpires stand directly behind the plate, they can sometimes be hit by pitches. This umpire is wearing the required protective equipment while officiating a baseball game.

young officials who want to move into the minor or major leagues. The umpires who complete training at these schools are often hired by the professional leagues.

Professional umpires work their way up through the leagues just like players do. You can expect to

BIG-LEAGUE FIRSTS

Here are some famous events in the long history of umpiring:

- 1876: William McLean officiates the first National League game on April 22, becoming the first professional umpire.
- 1903: The first modern World Series takes place, umpired by Hank O'Day and Thomas Connolly.
- 1951: Emmett Ashford becomes the first African American professional umpire.
- 1972: Bernice Gera becomes the first woman to umpire a professional baseball game.

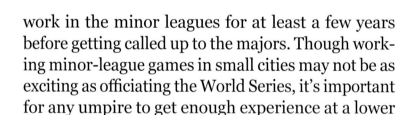

work in the minor leagues for at least a few years before getting called up to the majors. Though working minor-league games in small cities may not be as exciting as officiating the World Series, it's important for any umpire to get enough experience at a lower level. Then, when it's time to take on the big game, you'll be ready to make the call.

In addition to completing a training course at an umpire school, a potential umpire needs a high school degree or general equivalency diploma (GED), good eyesight, quick reflexes, and good coordination. An umpire must be able to remain calm in stressful situations, and, of course, they always have to be fair to all teams.

WHAT TO EXPECT

The pay you can expect to receive as an umpire will vary depending on the level at which you're working. When you first start off, you'll likely earn just a small amount per game, especially if you're working at middle and high school level games.

However, once you make it into the professional ranks, you'll start to make enough to live on. Beginning with single-A minor-league games and moving up to triple A and the major leagues, your compensation will increase at every professional milestone. In addition to your regular paycheck, you'll also receive benefits and steady raises, especially if you make it to the major leagues.

CHAPTER 4

SMOOTH SAILING

Cruise ships are often considered to be the height of luxury. From thrilling entertainment to all-you-can-eat buffets to having all your needs attended to, there are a lot of reasons people love to take cruise vacations. Have you ever considered, however, how much work is required to provide passengers with great experiences? If you find a job as a cruise director, you'll learn what it takes to keep people happy while they enjoy their vacation on the high seas.

WHAT YOU'LL DO

Working as a cruise director, you'll often find yourself wearing many hats at the same time. You'll have to be a manager, an entertainer, a customer service representative, and a friend. Broadly, you'll be responsible for planning all the activities and entertainment on the ship. This includes a wide variety of activities: sports, movies, trips to shore, special dinners, and

PART OF A TEAM

There are many people working as part of the cruise director's team. Working as a member of this team is a great way to learn before you move up to a director position. Here are some jobs you could do to gain experience:

- **Assistant cruise directors**: Help the director plan activities and make up the daily schedule.
- **Cruise staff**: Do a wide variety of jobs, including helping out with activities and games.
- **DJs**: Work with the cruise director to plan theme nights and pick out appropriate music.
- **Shore excursion managers**: Organize trips off the ship.
- **Social hosts/hostesses**: Greet and socialize with guests.

Part of a cruise director's job is organizing entertainment for passengers. You'll likely find yourself interacting with musicians of all kinds to create unique experiences for vacationers.

Cruise ships are crowded vessels packed with people who want to have a good time, all the time. If you become a cruise director, you'll be responsible for making sure everyone is entertained and treated well by your staff.

evening performances. The cruise director often hosts or introduces the shows each night. The overall most important job a cruise director has is making sure each and every passenger is happy and having a great vacation.

Being a cruise director is a demanding job. You often work 10 or more hours per day for many days

in a row. You need to get along well with all kinds of people—both your employees and your guests—and you must be polite, especially when a passenger is complaining. Even when you aren't on duty, you have to be friendly to passengers and crewmembers alike.

If all of that sounds exciting, then finding a job as a cruise director may be worth exploring. However, most people don't begin their cruise ship careers as directors. This is a job that requires a lot of experience and skill. Some people start as assistant cruise directors or have another job on the cruise director's staff.

WHAT YOU NEED

Cruise directors have to be committed to customer service. They need to be creative, organized, energetic, flexible, and, most of all, friendly. You can take classes to learn some of those skills, but many will have to be learned on the job. There are things you can do to prepare for a career as a cruise director, though. Take public speaking classes so you're comfortable talking in front of groups. Help plan a school trip so that you can learn what goes into scheduling and leading groups of people. Learning a foreign language can also be helpful, as cruise ships take on passengers of many different nationalities.

Do research on what cruise ships are like and what kinds of entry-level jobs are available. Try talking to travel agents or people who have worked on ships. Read travel magazines or the travel section of the newspaper. The more you know about cruise lines, vacation destinations, and the industry as a whole, the more likely you'll be a strong candidate when a job opens up.

You can also consider going to a travel school. The American Society of Travel Agents is a valuable online resource with a great deal of information about the business of traveling as well as educational opportunities for those in the industry. There are many travel programs around the country, and some of them specialize in training people for cruise ship jobs.

WHAT TO EXPECT

As managers with a lot of responsibilities, cruise directors are generally paid a substantial salary. On top of that, many cruise lines offer comprehensive benefits, including health insurance and retirement funding. Even a lower-level employee, such as an assistant cruise director, will receive many of the same benefits, but the salary will be lower.

In 2018, more than 29 million people took cruises. That's great news for anyone who wants to join this industry. On many cruise ships, there is one crewmember for every two or three passengers. With several thousand passengers per ship, it's clear that many crew members are needed.

Although a job as a cruise director isn't easy to get, you can work your way up to that position. Many people leave the cruise industry after a few years, or take a break from it, so there are often job openings. If you stay dedicated, you'll be able to climb the ranks and reach your dream occupation.

CHAPTER 5

DEDICATED DECKHANDS

If you love the water—whether it's the wide open ocean or a local river—there may be no better job for you than that of a deckhand. There are many different kinds of watercraft in the world, and they're all operated by crews of passionate deckhands. Though this work can be physically demanding and mentally tough, there's no better professional satisfaction than helping your ship have a successful journey.

WHAT YOU'LL DO

Most deckhand positions involve helping out on a boat. Deckhands can get jobs on many different types of boats, so specific duties can vary. On commercial fishing boats, for example, deckhands operate the fishing gear, such as nets and fishing line. They also help haul the fish into the boat. Once the fish are on the boat, deckhands clean and salt the fish and put the catch on ice for the long trip back to land.

Despite what you may have seen on TV, commercial fishing doesn't just take place on the high seas. Small vessels like this cruise through smaller bodies of water—and they need deckhands too.

Jobs like this can be easier to get because they don't require specific training or advanced education.

Cruise ship deckhand positions, on the other hand, aren't easy to get because most cruise ships hire crewmembers from outside the United States. However, small cruise ships and riverboats do hire American deckhands. On a riverboat or small cruise ship, a deckhand does everything from painting and cleaning to helping dock the boat.

On cargo ships, deckhands (sometimes called seamen) have to take on a lot of tasks. They sometimes steer the ship or stand watch, looking out for other ships and making sure their vessel is on course. They help dock the ship when it pulls into port. They may help load or unload cargo and may keep track of cargo during the ship's journey. Deckhands also make sure the ship is clean and in good working order.

Deckhands who work on private boats or yachts help sail the boat and make sure it's clean and running well. On boats with a small crew, deckhands sometimes also have other duties, such as cooking. Passenger ferries hire deckhands to help dock the boat, load cars and passengers, and collect money from passengers.

No matter what kind of ship you end up on, being a deckhand can be dangerous. Weather conditions, especially on the ocean, can sometimes be harsh. If the boat has a problem and is far from land, the crew needs to solve the problem on their own because there is no one else to help them. There is

DECKHAND DANGERS

Deckhands on commercial fishing vessels perform an important job, but their workplace can be an especially dangerous one. On the open water, ships heave and rock, making it hard to keep your footing. With cargo nets or metal cages full of fish swinging around on the deck, this can be a recipe for disaster. Decks are also naturally slick, especially during colder weather. An especially strong wave could knock you off your feet—and potentially over the edge of the deck. If you decide this is a career you want to pursue, make sure you're always following your captain's safety regulations and obey the orders of more experienced deckhands.

also the risk of falling overboard, particularly on a fishing boat or large cargo ship. If you want to work as a deckhand, make sure you always follow safety regulations to protect both yourself and the rest of the crew.

Some types of boats may be at sea—and away from land—for weeks or months at a time. Deckhands who work on cargo ships, fishing boats, or cruise ships typically work for several months straight and then have a month or two off. While they're at sea, they might be on duty for four hours, then off duty for eight hours, every day of the week for the entire voyage.

Deckhands on passenger ferries or boats in rivers and harbors commonly follow a more traditional

This deckhand is wearing some of the personal protective equipment (PPE) you can expect to see on most vessels. PPE includes helmets, gloves, safety vests, and more. This gear helps keep deckhands safe.

work schedule. They might work eight- or twelve-hour shifts, five days a week. They may work steadily for a week and then have a week off.

WHAT YOU NEED

Most deckhands receive on-the-job training. Experience on boats is the most important requirement for getting hired for many deckhand jobs. Some jobs on cargo ships or cruise ships require the deckhand to be officially licensed by the U.S. Coast Guard.

There are schools and programs that can train you for a career as a deckhand. You can also take courses offered by the U.S. Coast Guard or Canadian Coast Guard. Some companies have their own school and will train you when you're hired.

If you're interested in joining the armed forces, the U.S. Navy, Marine Corps, and Coast Guard can give you a lot of useful experience in your future career as a deckhand. This is a big commitment, however, and it's not necessary to have military training to work as a deckhand.

One of the most important aspects of any deckhand's qualifications is their fitness. To obtain most deckhand jobs, you'll need to be healthy and strong enough to perform your physically demanding duties. Patience is helpful as well because days at sea can be long. On almost any vessel, there will be times when you're not on duty and there is little to do. A deckhand must also be flexible enough to step in and do another crew member's job if someone is sick or injured. That's part of working as a team, which is another important quality for any deckhand. Crews must work together well so that everyone on board remains safe and the ship runs smoothly.

WHAT TO EXPECT

Because deckhand positions can vary so much, so does the typical compensation for people in this field. If you work on a fishing boat, you may make good money during fishing seasons and little when it's the offseason. If you're on a cruise ship, your paychecks will be steadier and more reliable, but these positions are hard to find. Before you commit to any deckhand job, find out how much the starting pay is and how much room there is for advancement.

Overall, working in this industry has its ups and downs. Total job opportunities in fishing and water transportation are expected to decline by 2 percent between 2018 and 2028. The need for deckhands goes up and down along with the economy. For example, if more goods are being shipped overseas, there will be a greater need for deckhands on cargo boats. However, if cruise liners have a bad year, they may cut positions. As in any business, however, if you can roll up your sleeves and get to work, there will likely be a job waiting for you.

CHAPTER 6

AIRBORNE ASSISTANCE

The pilots of commercial aircraft often get all the attention, but there's a whole crew of people that make everyday flights run smoothly. Though they aren't in charge of operating planes, flight attendants play an important role in the service and administration of a plane ride, whether it's a short jump between cities or a long-haul international journey. If you're interested in traveling the world—all expenses paid—while providing excellent customer service, becoming a flight attendant may be a dream come true.

WHAT YOU'LL DO

If you've ever been on an airplane, you've seen flight attendants greeting passengers at the door and getting bags safely packed into the storage bins. A flight attendant probably instructed you on safety procedures and likely served you drinks and passed out snacks.

The duties you see a flight attendant performing on the average flight are a big part of the job, but a lot more goes on behind the scenes. Before a flight, they make sure the plane is ready for passengers. Flight attendants help people if emergency situations arise, and they answer guest questions during flights. Flight attendants often work long days, and those days can become much longer if there is bad weather or a problem with the plane. They're typically on duty for more than one flight per day and often work nights, weekends, and holidays. Most flight attendants fly about 80 hours each month and spend about as much time working on the ground preparing planes or doing paperwork after a flight. Airlines commonly have a maximum number of hours a flight attendant can fly in a single month. Once the maximum number of hours is reached, a flight attendant will have the rest of the month off.

Service with a Smile is the motto for many flight attendants. If you pursue this career, you'll be expected to help passengers find their seats, address any concerns they may have, and make sure no one is breaking safety regulations—all with a friendly, professional attitude.

Flight attendants often start their careers on reserve. This means that they have scheduled days off and scheduled days on. They can get called at any time on their days on. They need to be able to get to the airport—ready to fly—on short notice. Most flight attendants live near the airport where they are based so they'll be able to get there quickly.

WHAT YOU NEED

Airlines mainly look for men and women who are healthy, clean-cut, mature, dependable, and friendly. Flight attendants need to be flexible, have a positive attitude, and be ready to deal professionally with any kind of situation. One of their most important jobs is dealing with passengers, so experience providing customer service to all kinds of people is very important.

A high school diploma or GED is required to get a job as a flight attendant. Some college education is preferred, but it's not necessary. Practical knowledge, such as first-aid training and experience with public speaking, can be very helpful. Any customer service experience is good, such as waiting tables or working in a hotel. Volunteer work as a tour guide can help to show an airline that you are skilled at working with people. Demonstrating that you have a positive attitude and good work ethic will take you a long way.

If you want to really get a leg up on your competitors, it can be helpful to learn a second language or spend time studying or traveling abroad. If you can't land a flight attendant position right away, try finding a job somewhere else at the airport, such as in ticketing. That will give you a chance to see how

AVIATION INFORMATION

Many people love air travel because it's faster than other methods. It's also getting easier and cheaper to fly, all of which is great news for the industry as a whole. If you want to pursue a career as a flight attendant, your prospects are good. More than 4.4 billion passengers flew in 2018, and this number isn't expected to decline. As more people fly, there will be increased need for in-flight service members. If you love traveling the world, there's even more good news: in 2018, the top five international flight locations were all located abroad, mainly in Asia. If you're willing to relocate, you should have no trouble finding consistent work traveling between exciting destinations.

the airlines work and will give you solid customer service experience.

When you are ready to apply for a job at an airline, be aggressive and keep at it. If you can, reach out to someone who already works for an airline to find out what kinds of qualities it's looking for in flight attendant candidates. They may also be able to tell you what kinds of questions to expect in an interview.

If you're hired by an airline, you'll receive extensive training for a month or more. During this time, you'll be taught first aid and emergency procedures, how to deal with difficult passengers, and how to serve food and drinks. Near the end of your training, you'll likely go on several practice flights.

Many people want to become flight attendants, which can make finding a position difficult. If you get started in airline ticketing, you can show your employer that you have good customer service skills—which can help you eventually land a job as a flight attendant.

WHAT TO EXPECT

Many flight attendants belong to unions, and these organizations help them acquire good benefits and salaries. According to the Bureau of Labor Statistics, the average flight attendant pay in 2018 was $56,000 per year.

One of the additional benefits of being a flight attendant is free or discounted travel. Flight attendants often get free flights on the airline that they work for and sometimes on other airlines too. They often get discounts on hotels, cruises, and rental cars as well. Some airlines even offer travel passes so a flight attendant can take their families on a free vacation.

There will be many opportunities for flight attendants between 2018 and 2028. There's expected to be a 10 percent increase in jobs during that time frame, which means the industry is growing much faster than the national average (5 percent).

CHAPTER 7

IN IT FOR THE LONG HAUL

Books, lettuce, video games, T shirts, milk—what do all of these products have in common? If you bought them at a local store, they were likely driven there by long-haul truck drivers. The people who operate large semitrucks are responsible for bringing all kinds of products to stores and warehouses all across the United States. As they drive, of course, they get the opportunity to travel around the country, see a lot of different cities and towns, and appreciate life on the open road.

WHAT YOU'LL DO

The goal of long-haul truck drivers is simple: getting cargo to its intended destination safely and on time. The job itself, however, is more complex than that. Before a trip, the driver checks the truck and cargo to make sure that everything is in good shape. When the trucker reaches the delivery location, they

Long-haul truck drivers make the highways crisscrossing the country from coast to coast their daily workplace. This is a job perfect for someone who likes traveling and doesn't mind being alone for extended periods of time.

sometimes help unload the cargo and then fill out paperwork about the trip.

Some truck drivers work for a trucking company and have regular routes. They may drive in a loop or a round trip between several cities. This takes a long time, and many truck drivers only get to be home for two or three days per week. Other drivers may be sent on different routes every time they make a trip. Truckers sometimes drive in teams, with one sleeping while the other is driving.

Some drivers work in trucks that they own. Owners must pay for everything related to the truck, which can be expensive. They must keep their truck in good condition and take as many jobs as possible in order to turn a profit. Because truck owners generally take on jobs more frequently, they get even less time at home than other truckers.

Trucks today are safer—and more comfortable—than they were in the past. Most trucks have heated and cooled cabins that have high-tech amenities and a bed or two. Most of the time, drivers sleep in their own trucks, unless the weather is bad. Most new trucks have Global Positioning Systems (GPS) that tell them exactly where they are at all times. GPS also helps them communicate with their dispatcher and other drivers.

WHAT YOU NEED

One of the main requirements for a trucker is being a skilled driver. You'll be responsible for delivering your cargo safely. Of course, you must love to drive too because that's what you'll be doing all day long.

If you're thinking about a career in long-haul trucking, you might want to take driver training and auto mechanic classes in high school. Some technical and vocational schools offer training courses specifically for truck drivers. When you get hired by a trucking company, you'll typically be sent to tractor-trailer school, so taking classes on your own is not always necessary.

Before you can drive for a long-haul trucking company, you'll need to get a commercial driver's license (CDL). This involves passing the CDL exam, which has a written portion and a driving portion. Trucking schools will help you to prepare for the exam.

The law requires that any tractor-trailer driver must be at least 21 years old. A good way to get experience before you reach that age is to drive smaller trucks for companies that make local deliveries within a city or state. Younger drivers can sometimes work as a truck driver's helper. Helpers drive part of the time and may help load and unload the truck.

WHAT TO EXPECT

Generally, tractor-trailer drivers are paid by the mile. Though this means your pay will sometimes vary, the wage generally balances out to be about $21 per hour.

If you own your own truck, you'll set your own pay. You may make more money on paper than someone working for a trucking company, but keep in mind that you'll also have to pay to maintain your vehicle.

If you find work as a local delivery driver, you can expect to earn a little less, about $14 per hour. Drivers in these positions are usually paid by the hour and get overtime if they work more than 40 hours per week.

There will be many opportunities for truck drivers for the foreseeable future. Trucks can often deliver cargo faster than railroads and other types of transportation, so the industry is expected to grow. Overall, its

The first step in your trucking career is getting a commercial driver's license. To earn this certification, you have to prove that you have the knowledge and skills required to operate complex vehicles like semitrucks.

projected 5 percent growth between 2018 and 2028 is even with the U.S. average.

CHAPTER 8

SHOWING OFF

When people think about sales jobs, they may picture a dishonest car dealer or a pushy employee in a retail store. However, there's a lot more to the business of selling products than these stereotypes suggest. Models who wear the latest fashions for advertisements are part of the sales force, as are the product demonstrators who hand out samples at your local grocery store. Though life in this industry can be challenging, no matter your position, if you stick with it and show your skills, you may get opportunities to travel around the country or around the world.

WHAT YOU'LL DO

The goal of most models is to convince people to buy things, from clothes, makeup, and jewelry to food and many other types of products. Fashion models are photographed for advertisements in magazines, newspapers, or billboards. Many models appear in clothing catalogs. Others are filmed

Though the profession of modeling can take on many different forms—including walking the latest fashions on the runway—they all share a common goal: showing off a product or promoting a brand.

for television commercials. Some do live modeling, walking the runways at fashion shows or in department stores. Top models are known around the world and some even have their own clothing lines or fitness programs.

Some models specialize in one type of work. For instance, they model only specific parts of their body. Hand models, for example, advertise rings or nail polish. Some work as models for artists or sculptors.

Models can work all over the world and rarely work for just one company. Their jobs can last from a few hours to a few days. Most models don't have a regular schedule. They may work 10 days in a row but then have the next week off. Sometimes, their jobs are glamorous, like modeling at a fashion show in Milan, Italy, or posing for a magazine photo shoot in Hawaii. Other times, they must stand in the cold while a photographer waits for the sun to come out from behind a cloud. They must be patient while stylists fix their hair and makeup.

Product promoters or demonstrators have a similar job to models: they're trying to interest people in buying a certain product. They go to stores, state fairs, car shows, and other places to show their product and tell consumers about it. Sometimes, product promoters give out free samples or gifts to customers. They may even be asked to wear costumes or wave sign boards in public to advertise new products. Product promoters can work for department stores, market research firms, or the company that makes the product that they are promoting.

As with models, product promoters and demonstrators have fairly irregular schedules. They may work nights and weekends at state fairs or trade shows all over the country. While they're working, they may be on duty for many hours and may have to stand or talk for long periods of time. However, the chance to travel and the opportunity to meet lots of people make it worthwhile to many people who become product promoters.

WHAT YOU NEED

Models don't need any special training or formal education to begin their career. However, becoming a model is not something that everyone can do. Models need to have the right look to show off a company's products. In general, companies are looking for people who have the confidence and appearance to best highlight their products.

If you think you have what it takes, modeling schools are one way to get training and experience before you join the workforce. Going to a school is not always a requirement, though. Many modeling agencies will give their models all the training they need, so paying for an expensive school isn't necessary. Getting an agent is an important first step to beginning your modeling career. Agents can help you to get work and advise you on how to advance. However, they also typically take a cut of your pay, so be careful before signing on with an agency.

To become a product promoter or demonstrator, the only requirements are a high school degree and excellent communication skills. Most product promoters get their training on the job, and they're often trained again each time they get a new product. The stores or companies they work for teach them about the goods or services they're promoting. A demonstrator, for example, sometimes needs to learn special skills so they can cook up a frozen meal to give out free samples.

Being able to speak well and convince people to buy your product are the most important parts of the job of a product promoter. To prepare, it's a good idea to take public speaking courses or drama classes. These will help you to become comfortable speaking in front of groups.

If you become a product promoter, you'll be expected to be outgoing and lively. You'll have to be willing to approach people you don't know—and willing to accept a lot of rejection from people who aren't interested in what you're selling.

WHAT TO EXPECT

Because you don't need any advanced education or special skills to work as a product promoter, the starting pay is low. The positions are either paid a flat hourly rate or they work on commission. This means they can earn extra money by meeting sales goals.

In addition to being a difficult industry to get into, modeling can be financially tough. The Bureau of Labor Statistics reported that the average salary for a model in 2018 was less than $24,000. However, top models can earn much more. Some job opportunities may also give models bonuses, such as designer clothing. It's important to note as well that most modeling agencies take between 10 and 20 percent of their clients' earnings.

While demonstrators will always be needed to showcase new products, job opportunities declined in the early 2000s. Though it's expected to increase again, this job's outlook is worth monitoring.

It's expected to be very difficult to find modeling work in the future. The industry's jobs are expected to decline by 10 percent between 2018 and 2028. If this is a path you want to pursue, make sure you have a backup plan in case you encounter professional challenges.

CHAPTER 9

CAMERA REPORTING

There's an old saying that a picture is worth a thousand words. As a photojournalist, you'd be telling important newsworthy stories without ever putting pen to paper. If you work for a national publication, you may be asked to travel to Russia to photograph a political meeting or to Africa to support an article on poachers. If you work freelance, you can travel anywhere in the world, hoping to capture a good story from behind the lens. Though you may face obstacles in this field—such as an irregular schedule, long hours, and being woken up in the middle of the night—once you see your images in print or online, you'll know you picked the right occupation.

WHAT YOU'LL DO

The long and short of photojournalism is that you're expected to capture newsworthy moments on camera. Photojournalists tell a story with images.

Photojournalists cover many types of stories. Someone who works for a local newspaper may photograph car accidents or meetings of community organizations. A photojournalist who works for a national newsmagazine may find themselves covering peace talks in the Middle East or a presidential election. Sports photographers might travel to cities all over the country capturing pictures of great catches or amazing goals.

As a photojournalist, you may work for a single publication or agency, or you may choose to be a freelancer. This means that you'd work for many different companies or publications, doing single jobs at a time. If you really like to travel, being a freelance photojournalist may be the right option for you.

Another way to get some guaranteed travel time is to work for a major national or international publication. Because these newspapers and magazines

In addition to fun and exciting photography opportunities, many photojournalists also travel to dangerous areas to photograph warfare and conflict.

cover global news, they must send journalists and photographers all over the world. Photojournalists employed by sports photo agencies also cover a lot of ground. As a sports photographer covering professional baseball, for example, your typical day might start with getting up early to travel to the field and check your equipment. In the afternoon, you'll get your cameras set up in the ballpark. You might socialize with the other reporters or even the players. During the game, you'll be busy capturing the action on the field. However, most of the hard work happens after the game. You'll want to check the shots you got during the game and pick the best ones. If you work for a newspaper, you'll rush to send the pictures to the newsroom. Your colleagues need to get the photos so that they can get them printed in the morning edition.

WHAT YOU'LL NEED

There are many ways to get started in photojournalism. For example, you can work as an assistant to a professional photographer. Working at a photo lab or photo studio is another way to gain experience behind the lens. A summer job or internship at a

Photojournalism used to be as simple as taking a great shot, developing the film, and delivering the goods. Nowadays, however, you'll likely be responsible for digitally editing and cleaning up your shots. Knowledge of advanced image editing software will help you find a job.

local newspaper or magazine can teach you what the job is really like.

If you land a photojournalism job, you'll be responsible for all the equipment you might use. It's important to gain experience with digital cameras, image editing software, and other photography gear, such as tripods and lenses. Take any photography classes your school offers, or investigate local community programs. Joining the photo staff of your school yearbook or newspaper is also a good place to learn more about photography.

WHAT TO EXPECT

Photography in general isn't known as a high-paying career, but photojournalists often make more money than other photographers. The best way to ensure a steady income is to find a permanent full-time job at a newspaper or magazine, but these jobs are getting harder to find as companies hire more freelancers.

Becoming a freelance photojournalist can be an appealing option. You'd be able to set your own schedule, take on the jobs you want, and be your own boss. However, there are also downsides. You'd have to rely on work popping up, and you'd probably experience months during which you have little work. This can be risky. If you spend this downtime learning additional image-related skills, such as capturing video or drone photography, you may find yourself operating a busy freelance business.

CHAPTER 10

TAKING MEASURES

Have you ever wondered how huge construction projects get started? Most of the time, they begin with a team of surveyors and surveying technicians, who use special tools to observe and measure land, sea, and air space. This can be as basic as writing down the measurements of an open city lot or as complex as noting the topography of a totally undeveloped parcel of land. Some positions in this field require a lot of travel, whether locally or to faraway locations, to take measures. If you're interested in math and you're a detail-oriented worker, you may find success as a surveying technician.

WHAT YOU'LL DO

Surveying technicians work on teams called survey parties. They operate the equipment and tools that measure the area that they are surveying. They take detailed notes, make sketches of the area, and record all the data in a computer.

Because survey teams are often working in undeveloped areas, they have to carry bulky equipment to and from the survey site.

A lot of a surveying technician's day is spent outside, and they often have to travel for their work. Some sites may be close enough for the technician to drive

to, but sometimes the job requires long-distance travel. Occasionally, a surveying technician will temporarily move to the survey site.

Being a surveying technician is often physically demanding. Technicians generally have to stand for long periods of time and walk great distances. Surveying equipment tends to be heavy, and technicians must carry all the gear they need to wherever their site is located. Additionally, if you take this job, you'll find yourself outside in all kinds of weather, from searing summers to freezing winters. Surveying technicians typically work a standard workweek, though certain jobs may require overtime.

After getting several years of on-the-job experience, a surveying technician can become a senior surveying technician. After that, the next professional step is to take exams to become licensed as a surveyor.

GETTING THE PARTY TOGETHER

A land survey party collects information the surveyor needs from a particular location. There are typically about four to eight people in the party. Here are some of the party's members:

- **Party chief (a land surveyor or senior survey technician)**: This person supervises the group and makes sure measurements are accurate.
- **Surveying technician**: This person helps the party chief, operates equipment, and takes notes.
- **Assistant**: This person helps operate the surveying equipment.
- **Helper**: This person carries equipment, clears the land to make it easier to set up the equipment, and sets up traffic warnings if necessary.

WHAT YOU NEED

On-the-job training is often the best way for surveying technicians to get experience. If you're interested in this job, you can get started by working as an apprentice to a surveying team. Since surveying teams often have more work during warmer months, they may hire high school students for the summer.

You can start training for a career in this field as early as high school. Though most schools don't teach specific surveying courses, you can take more general classes to get a solid background. Math classes such as algebra, geometry, and trigonometry are recommended. Computer science classes will help you to prepare for working with the equipment that surveyors use. Classes in drafting or mechanical drawing will help you learn technical drawing skills.

If you want more formal training, there are vocational schools that offer programs that teach students surveying skills or surveying engineering technology. If you earn an associate's degree from a vocational school, you'll be more likely to start working at a higher salary level than if you had started working directly out of high school.

Surveying technicians are frequently employed by architects and engineers or by construction companies. State and local governments and government agencies, such as the Forest Service or the U.S. Geological Survey, also hire surveying technicians.

WHAT TO EXPECT

If you can make it into the field, you'll likely be able to earn a good yearly salary. Surveying technicians who work for local, state, or federal governments earn more than those who work for engineering or architectural firms. The most potential for earning, however, is working for companies that provide utilities.

According to the Bureau of Labor Statistics, jobs for surveying technicians are expected to grow at an average rate of about 5 percent between 2018 and 2028. As construction increases, so, too, will demand for surveying technicians. Surveying technicians also

ALL-TERRAIN SURVEYING

Surveys aren't just done on land. Here are some of the techniques surveyors use to map on land, in the air, and underwater.

- Land surveying technicians use tools such as a GPS, which uses radio signals from satellites to give precise locations.
- Surveying can be done from the air by attaching a camera to the bottom of a plane or a drone. The aircraft flies over the area being surveyed and takes many pictures. The pictures are then put together with a computer to produce an accurate image.
- Underwater surveys are conducted using sonar. This technology uses sound waves to find and identify objects and the terrain.

help measure land for environmentally protected areas, so there will be a lot of options and openings if you want to pursue this career.

CHAPTER 11

PERFORMING ON THE SEAS

Cruise ships carry passengers all over the world. On these lengthy sea voyages, paying customers need to be entertained. Most cruise liners, both big and small, employ performers—from dancers to singers to comedians and more—to keep their passengers happy. This field can be highly competitive, as working on a cruise ship is seen as a luxurious lifestyle, but if you have a knack for keeping people entertained, you can find a place to thrive on the open seas.

WHAT YOU'LL DO

Entertainment on cruise ships is highly variable. Because the average cruise vacation lasts about a week, most liners search out diverse performances. After all, people won't want to watch the same show for a week straight. If you have a talent for singing, music, dancing, comedy, or even juggling—and you'd enjoy traveling the world—you may find your dream job on a cruise ship.

There are many different kinds of jobs for entertainers on cruise ships. Most nights, there's a large show featuring dancers, singers, and musicians. There are also solo acts, such as shows by magicians or comedians. Musicians can be part of an orchestra that plays while guests dance. They can also be in smaller bands that provide background music during an activity.

Many entertainers take part in the big shows that are often the highlight of the evening for cruise passengers. These shows also need costume designers, lighting specialists, choreographers, and producers.

Entertainers on cruise ships work hard, but they also have free time to enjoy the ship. Most performances take place in the evening, and—except for a rehearsal in the afternoon—entertainers can go ashore or relax on the ship most of the day, much like the paying passengers.

In addition to their regular shows, entertainers sometimes have other duties. They may greet passengers, help out with activities and games, or perform in smaller shows. Entertainers are often expected to talk with passengers, so you need to be friendly and outgoing if you want this job.

If you have skills as an entertainer, you love the idea of traveling, but you're not sure that life on a cruise ship is for you, consider working at a resort. Many resorts all over the world have nightly shows to entertain their guests. These programs may

The life of a cruise ship entertainer can be glamorous. Whether your talent is acting, singing, dancing, or anything else, you'll be performing in front of hundreds or thousands of passengers every time your ship heads out.

feature singers, dancers, or musicians. Musicians are often hired to play at the pool or beach to entertain the guests during the day as well.

WHAT YOU NEED

No matter what your performance talent is, the most important thing to do is practice your skill. Perform in plays, musicals, or talent shows. Practice will help you to develop your talent. It will also help you to gain confidence working in front of a crowd.

While you're working on your act, you can also research cruise lines. Find out what kinds of shows different cruise companies like to put on. You can also research agencies that represent entertainers for cruise lines. Once you've done your research and your skills are ready to be put to the test, make a recording to show off your talent. Keep the tape short, and make sure it looks professional. Cruise ship entertainers can apply and audition in person,

As an entertainer, you'll be sharing the ship with other passengers for the length of the voyage. If you put on a good show, guests may recognize you and want to chat or take pictures. You should always treat passengers with respect.

but it's common to show off your talents through a video recording.

STARTING YOUR ENTERTAINMENT CAREER

When it comes time for you to put your entertainment skills to the test, there are many people to whom you can reach out. The manager of a cruise ship may be able to give you advice on what kind of act to work on. They may also be able to direct you to a talent agency that represents many of their previous hires. Agencies often work closely with cruise lines and help ships find entertainers. A producer puts shows together, hiring entertainers as well as costume designers and sound and light technicians. The producer then sells the whole show to a cruise line. Getting on board with an agency or a production company can help get you on board a cruise ship.

WHAT TO EXPECT

As in any form of show business, the compensation for cruise ship entertainers varies widely. It's often based on the cruise line that employs you, the skills you're bringing to the table, and how much a ship needs a person of your specific skills. However, it's worth noting that you'll likely receive good health benefits regardless of the cruise line, and you'll be getting paid to do something you love.

As cruise ships continue to rise in popularity as a vacation option, so, too, will more entertainer positions open up. Passengers will always need to be entertained while at sea, and if you're committed to finding a job in this industry, there should be work available.

CHAPTER 12

GROUP TRAVELING

Of all the available jobs that combine travel with professional fulfillment, tour guide may be the most obvious. In addition to being paid to go all over the world, if you pursue a career as a guide, you'll be able to share the excitement and enjoyment of traveling with others. Even if you don't find a position that allows you to travel internationally, leading tour groups around your city can still be a satisfying occupation.

WHAT YOU'LL DO

Tour guides can go by several names, and their tasks can vary. They're sometimes called tour managers or tour escorts. They may live on location and meet their group at the airport or travel with clients to their destination. They help everyone in the group go through customs smoothly. All tour guides travel with their group, making sure everyone gets where they're supposed to be on time and in one piece.

Tour guides are commonly on duty 24 hours a day, 7 days a week when they're leading a tour. They're typically the first ones to wake up and the last ones to go to sleep. A tour guide double-checks everything before the day's events and keeps double-checking all the arrangements during the tour.

Managing all these responsibilities can be stressful. Tour guides put in long days, and even if they're tired, they have to be able to solve any problems that come up along the way. This can be something as simple as looking for a lost suitcase, or it can be as serious as finding a group member who's wandered off.

One of the most important jobs that a tour guide has is making sure that all the customers on the tour are enjoying their vacation. Tour guides are paid to make sure that things go smoothly and to ensure that customers get to experience a destination to its fullest.

You've probably seen tour guides like this at an airport or train station, waiting to pick up their clients. As the first face tour groups see when they arrive at their destination, you must always be friendly and professional.

Not all tour guides travel with one particular group. Some guides work in a specific city and will give driving or walking tours of that location. If you want to be this type of guide, you'll need to know a lot about a particular location. More importantly, you must want to share your love of that location with others. Other guides have a specialized knowledge of an entire country or have a skill that helps them lead an unusual type of trip, such as a safari. "Step-on" guides are hired by a tour company to give a talk or a tour to a visiting group. These guides might get on a tour bus and give a lecture as the bus drives to various locations around a city.

Tour guides may spend several months straight leading groups of tourists, then have a month or two off to rest up or travel on their own. Tour guides sometimes get to travel to a new place for free to check it out and become familiar with it before leading a group there.

WHAT YOU NEED

There are tour guide schools and training programs, but gaining  hands-on experience is often the best training possible for an aspiring guide. In addition to on-the-job training, a tour guide needs to be organized, responsible, and ready to deal with any situation. Helping plan school trips or managing a sports team at your high school might help you to develop those skills.

If you want to lead tours, you'll also need good customer service and interpersonal skills. Volunteering as a guide in a local museum or working in a hotel

The world is full of incredible landmarks that attract tourists. It's only natural that these people look to professional guides to learn more about iconic buildings, exotic places, and local history.

or restaurant will help you polish your people skills. You may also find it beneficial to study a foreign language, to learn as much history as possible, and to take a public speaking class. All of these talents will make your résumé pop if you're applying to work at a touring company.

When you think you're ready to become a tour guide, some companies will train you by sending you on tours with an experienced guide. You'd assist the guide and learn about the place you're visiting. Watch the guide closely to see how they interact with the people on the tour and handle problems that come up. Soon, you'll be ready to lead a tour on your own.

WHAT TO EXPECT

The amount of money you can make as a tour guide varies greatly. Some tour guides are paid a regular salary, even when they're not out leading a tour. Other guides lead tours only during particular seasons and make less money as a result.

In addition to your paycheck, if you're a tour guide, you can expect to get tips from your customers—especially if they're satisfied. Additional benefits include having all your expenses paid while you're leading the tour. You may also get to occasionally travel for free when you're scoping out potential new tour sites.

The Bureau of Labor Statistics estimates that tour guide positions will increase by 7 percent between 2018 and 2028, making this career path a viable long-term option if you have the desire to make it work.

CHAPTER 13

WORKING THE RAILS

The system of interconnected train lines and railways used to be one of America's greatest treasures. In modern times, fewer people are using trains to get around. That doesn't mean, however, that working as a train conductor—whether for passenger or freight trains—is a dead-end career. On the contrary, it can be a rewarding position if you have the work ethic and skill to break into the field.

WHAT YOU'LL DO

Conductors can work on two types of trains: passenger or freight. Passenger trains carry people from point A to point B, whether they're traveling cross-country or just getting to work. Freight trains carry all kinds of cargo. Conductors who work on them have to keep track of the items. They have to know where each piece of cargo is being dropped off and where the train has to pick up more.

Passenger train conductors like this are responsible for making sure those traveling by train get on and off safely.

Conductors of passenger trains have different responsibilities. Their job is to take tickets, hand out schedules, help passengers, and announce train stops. On some passenger trains, there are assistant conductors who collect tickets and help passengers with their baggage.

Being a freight conductor is hard work. Since this style of conductor spends a lot of time outside, people in this position must be able to comfortably handle different weather and climate conditions. It may be sizzling hot outside but icy cold inside the cars. Freight conductors sometimes help hook and unhook the cargo cars, and climbing on and off the cars can be dangerous. Freight trains don't run on regular daily schedules, so conductors are often called to work on short notice. Because freight trains travel long distances, freight conductors may be away from home for many nights in a row.

Passenger trains have a more regular schedule, so passenger conductors typically know when they will be expected to work. However, like freight conductors, passenger conductors often have to work nights, weekends, and holidays.

WHAT YOU NEED

If you're interested in becoming a conductor, all you need is a high school degree or GED. Most railroads will provide training after you're hired, offering classes and on-the-job experience. Conductors rarely start at that position, often they start as brake operators and are promoted to conductor when there's an opening. As an entry-level railway worker, you'll likely have an irregular schedule. You'll be asked to fill in for other workers who are out sick or on vacation. You'll eventually get a regular schedule, and after that, you can start looking upward to conductor opportunities.

You don't need any special skills to be a freight conductor, but you do need to be in good health and have good eyesight. If you want to be a conductor on a passenger train, you'll need good people skills, so it helps to have some customer service experience.

Some conductors work for train touring companies that give modern tourists a glimpse into the past, showing what the golden age of railroads looked like through scenic journeys by train.

WHAT TO EXPECT

Most conductors, whether they work on freight or passenger trains, are offered generous starting salaries. Nearly all conductors belong to unions and receive good benefits, including health care and retirement plans. They also get paid for working over-time, which is sometimes required in this industry.

Unfortunately, jobs for conductors are expected to decline slightly between 2018 and 2028. Railroads are still used to transport freight, but newer trains need fewer people to operate them. Additionally, passenger travel by rail—especially in the United States—is quite low outside of commuter trains. Competition for conductor jobs will be tough, as fewer trains running means less demand for the job.

CHAPTER 14

HELPING OTHERS GET THERE

You're passionate about travel, and you know others would love to see the world as well. What if you could help people get where they want to go? You can if you pursue a career as a travel agent. In this position, you'll not only get to travel yourself, you'll also get to make others' sightseeing dreams come true.

WHAT YOU'LL DO

A travel agent's job ranges from simple to complex. They may help someone book a flight or get a rental car for a trip to Disney World. They may help a traveler book a worldwide cruise, with multiple stops and transportation methods. These agents specialize in leisure (or vacation) travel. Other agents specialize in travel for businesspeople. This is called corporate travel. These agents help companies make reservations or plan meetings for their employees.

One of a travel agent's main goals is helping clients find the perfect vacation. It helps to have a lot of firsthand travel experience.

In addition to picking between leisure and business travel, agents may specialize in a particular type of travel. Some may help customers book cruises. Others work on site for a large company or university, helping them book travel for their employees or students.

If you love to travel, you'll be happy to hear that the best part of the job for most travel agents is that they often get to travel for free or at a reduced rate. They sometimes go on familiarization trips that help them get to know a country, a new hotel, or a new cruise line. These trips are commonly paid for by airlines, hotels, or cruise lines. These companies hope that if the travel agent enjoys the trip, they'll recommend the company to their clients. Although these trips are not really vacations, they're a good opportunity to see new places all over the world.

WHAT YOU NEED

There are many ways to get started as a travel agent. There are schools that offer full-time or night and weekend courses for people who want to become travel agents. However, you don't need any advanced education or vocational training to make it in the field.

Most travel agencies look for computer and office-related skills in job applicants. One way to get started is to find any job where you have to do office work, such as filing and photocopying. You can also train by planning simple trips. Once you have some experience in the office, you can begin planning more complex trips. Some agencies will hire high school students to work afternoons or weekends, so keep an eye out for local job postings.

If you're hired as a travel agent, you can expect to receive a lot of on-the-job training before you're ready to book trips for clients. Travel software can be complex, so having a strong computer background and a willingness to learn new systems will help you get ready faster.

Learning about other countries can also help a travel agent in their job. Customers will likely ask you where you'd recommend traveling based on a lists of interests, likes, and dislikes. The more you know about cultures and opportunities at destinations around the globe, the better you'll be able to help someone book the perfect vacation.

One of the most important things a travel agent needs to be able to do is listen. It is essential to understand what the client really wants. If the travel agent succeeds in making customers happy, they'll come back again.

WHAT TO EXPECT

With the rise of the internet and free, easy-to-use consumer travel software, travel agencies have been hit with hard times. In fact, the number of jobs for travel agents is expected to decline by 6 percent between 2018 and 2028. If you do make it into the field, however, you can expect to make a reasonable salary; the Bureau of Labor Statistics reports that in 2018, the average pay for a travel agent was around $39,000 per year.

As the industry shrinks, however, it's likely that pay will become less reliable. Travel agencies are expected to make less money, which means their employees must also make less. However, if you can look past the uncertain future in the field, you can find yourself a rewarding career that allows you to travel far and wide—and help others do so too.

agency A company that helps people get work in a certain industry.

amenity Something that makes life more convenient or enjoyable.

catapult A device for launching an airplane, typically from the deck of an aircraft carrier.

choreographer Someone who arranges and directs dances.

civilian A person not on active duty in the military.

commercial Describing something done in order to make a profit.

ecotourism Travel to areas of natural or ecological interest, usually with a guide, to learn about the environment.

excursion A short trip off a cruise ship.

extensive Thorough or complete.

freight Goods or cargo transported in a ship, an airplane, a truck, a train, or another vehicle.

internship A job that allows someone to get work experience in a particular field.

milestone A significant point or achievement.

officiate To work as a referee or an umpire.

sonar A device for locating objects under water using sound waves.

survey To measure the size, shape, and position of an area of land, air, or water.

tip A wage given in addition to a worker's salary to show appreciation for the job done.

topography The natural features in an area.

tripod A three-legged stand for a camera or another piece of equipment.

union A group of workers who join together for better wages and working conditions.

yacht A ship used for pleasure sailing or racing.

FOR MORE INFORMATION

Adventure Travel Trade Association (ATTA)

14751 North Kelsey Street, Suite 105 PMB 604
Monroe, WA 98272
(360) 805-3131
Website: https://www.adventuretravel.biz
Facebook: @adventuretraveltradeassociation
Instragram: @poweredbyadventure_
Twitter: @adventuretweets

Formed in 1990, this professional organization connects travel agents, local guides, tourism officials, and other people who contribute to adventure travel worldwide. Its website features industry news and information.

Fisheries and Oceans Canada

200 Kent Street, Station 13E228
Ottawa, ON K1A 0E6
Canada
(613) 993-0999
Website: www.dfo-mpo.gc.ca/index-eng.htm
Facebook: @FisheriesOceansCanada
Instagram: @fisheriesoceanscan

A division of the Canadian government, this agency protects the country's waterways and fishing areas by working together with private corporations and individuals.

The International Ecotourism Society (TIES)

Website: https://ecotourism.org
Facebook: @ecotravelpage
Instagram: @ties_ecotourism

Twitter: @ecotravel
A nonprofit organization founded in 1990, TIES works to expand the global ecotourism industry. It offers training courses and certifications, and it helps bring members together.

National Association of Sports Officials (NASO)
2017 Lathrop Avenue
Racine, WI 52405
(262) 632-5460
Website: https://www.naso.org
Facebook and Twitter: @NASOofficiating
NASO is a professional organization that supports officials for all kinds of sports, all over the world. Its site has training information and other resources.

National Outdoor Leadership School (NOLS)
284 Lincoln Street
Lander, WY 82520
(800) 710-6657
Website: https://www.nols.edu/en
Facebook: @NOLS
Instagram and Twitter: @NOLSedu
This training organization helps young people improve their leadership and outdoors skills. It offers hands-on education courses that would be a great fit for an aspiring wilderness tour guide or anyone who wants to learn more about leadership and management in a natural environment.

Ontario Trucking Association (OTA)
555 Dixon Road
Toronto, ON M9W 1H8
Canada
(866) 713-4188
Website: http://ontruck.org
Facebook: @OTA Premier Events
Twitter: @OnTruck
The OTA is a professional organization that represents, educates, and connects truckers from all across Ontario. Its website offers news and information about the industry.

Professional Truck Driver Institute (PTDI)
13791 East Rice Place, Suite 114
Aurora, CO 80015
(720) 575-7444
Website: http://www.ptdi.org
Facebook: @PTDI86
The PTDI was formed to help new truck drivers learn the rules and regulations of trucking. Its website can help direct you toward classes and more information on this industry.

FOR FURTHER READING

Dev, Bal Krishan. *Managing Cruise Ship Tourism*. New Delhi, India: Random Publications, 2019.

Institute for Career Research. *Career as a Travel Agent: Tour Packager*. Chicago, IL: Institute for Career Research, 2015.

Liebman, Daniel. *I Want to Be a Truck Driver*. Richmond Hill, Canada: Firefly Books, 2018.

Loomis, Jim. *All Aboard: The Complete North American Train Travel Guide*. Chicago, IL: Chicago Review Press, 2015.

Manning, Nick, and Kerin Ramirez. *How to Be a Tour Guide: The Essential Training Manual for Tour Managers and Tour Guides*. New York, NY: Pronoun, 2017.

Pawlewski, Sarah. *Careers: The Graphic Guide to Finding the Perfect Job for You*. New York, NY: DK Publishing, 2015.

Stewart, Wayne. *You're the Umpire: Mind-Boggling Questions to Test Your Baseball Knowledge*. New York, NY: Skyhorse Publishing, 2019.

A

adventure travel specialist, working as an, 5, 6, 7, 9, 10
agency
entertainment, 74
news, 60
talent, 76
aircraft carriers, 12, 14, 17, 18
aircraft launch and recovery specialist, working as a, 12, 13, 14, 17, 18

B

baseball, 19, 21, 22, 24, 61
basic training, 17

C

cargo, 13, 34, 35, 47–48, 49, 50, 83, 85
cargo ships, 34–35, 37, 38
catapults, 12, 14
choreographers, 72
commercial aircraft, 39
commercial driver's license (CDL), 49
commercial fishing boats, jobs on, 32, 35
compensation
of conductors, 87
of cruise ship directors, 30
of cruise ship entertainers, 76
of deckhands, 38
of flight attendants, 45
of military, 18
of models, 58
of surveyors, 69
of tour guides, 82
of travel agents, 93
of umpires, 25
cruise director, working as a, 26, 27, 28, 29, 30, 31
cruise ships, 26, 29, 30, 31, 34, 35, 37, 38, 71–72, 74–75, 76
working as an entertainer on, 71, 72, 74, 76
customer service, 4, 26, 29, 39, 42–43, 80–81, 86

D

dancers, 71, 72, 74
deckhand, working as a,
  32, 34, 37–38
  cargo ship, 34, 37, 38
  cruise ship, 34, 37
  dangers of, 35
  passenger ferry, 34, 35
  training, 37

E

ecotourism, 9
emergencies, 6, 10, 40,
  43
engineer, 13, 14, 69

F

first-aid classes, 10,
  42, 43
flight attendant, work-
  ing as a, 39, 40,
  41–42, 43, 45
flight deck, 12–13, 17
freelancer, working as
  a, 59, 60, 64

G

Global Positioning Sys-
  tems (GPS), 48, 70

government agencies, 69
growth rate
  in modeling, 58
  in trucking, 50–51
  of surveying techni-
    cians, 69
  of tour guides, 82
  of travel agents, 93

I

internship, 62–63

J

jet, 12, 14
  noise of, 13–14

L

long-haul truck driver,
  working as a, 46, 47,
  48, 49, 50

M

military careers, 12, 13,
  14–15, 17, 18, 37
model, working as a,
  52, 53, 54, 55, 58
modeling agencies,
  55–56, 58
modeling school, 55

musicians, 72, 74

P

passenger ferries, 34, 35–36
photojournalist, working as a, 59, 60, 61, 62, 63, 64
planes, 12–13, 14, 17, 39, 40, 70
product promoter/demonstrator, working as a, 52, 54–55, 56, 57
public speaking classes, 10, 29, 42, 56, 81

R

recruiter, 16, 18
resorts, 72

S

safety, 13
   regulations, 35, 39
schedule, 35–36
   of deckhands, 35–36
   of flight attendants, 41
   of freight train conductors, 85
   of models, 54

of passenger train conductors, 85
of photojournalists, 59, 64
of product promoters, 55
of railway workers, 86
of umpires, 21
sports photo agencies, 61
sports photographers, 60, 61–62
surveying courses, 68
surveying equipment, 67, 68
surveying team, 68
surveying technician, working as a, 65, 66, 67, 68, 69–70
surveyor, 65, 67, 68, 69
surveys, 70

T

talent agency, 76
teamwork, 4, 7, 10
tips, 11, 82
topography, 65
tour guide, working as a, 42, 77, 78, 79, 80, 82

train conductor, working as a, 83, 84, 85, 86, 87, 88
training
    for adventure guides, 9, 10
    for deckhands, 34, 37
    driver, 49
    first-aid, 42
    for flight attendants, 43
    for a job on a cruise ship, 30
    military, 14–15, 17, 37
    for models, 55
    on-the-job, 4, 68, 92
    for product promoters, 56
    for railroad jobs, 86
    for surveyors, 68, 69
    for tour guides, 80, 82
    for travel agents, 92
    umpire, 22–23, 24
trains
    freight, 83, 85, 86, 87, 88
    lines, 83
    types of, 83
travel agencies, 92, 93
    jobs at, 92
    outlook for, 93

travel agent, working as a, 30, 89, 91, 92, 93

U
umpire, working as an, 19, 21, 22, 23, 24, 25
umpire school, 24
unions, 45, 87–88

Y
yachts, 34

ABOUT THE AUTHOR

Morgan Williams lives in New York with her husband and two corgis, Tate and Isabelle. She enjoys traveling the world to take in different cultures and cuisines. She's gone on adventures in Japan, Peru, and Iran.

CREDITS